THE ART OF TATTING

Our work is for human eternities!

Mag 1910

Carmen Sylva

PLATE I

H.M. THE QUEEN OF ROUMANIA

THE
ART OF TATTING

BY

KATHARIN L. HOARE

WITH AN INTRODUCTION BY

H.M. THE QUEEN OF ROUMANIA

B. T. Batsford Ltd · London

First published 1910 by Longmans, Green & Co.
This edition published 1988

ISBN 0 7134 6035 0

Printed and bound in Great Britain
by Butler & Tanner Ltd, Frome and London
for the Publisher
B. T. Batsford Ltd
4 Fitzhardinge Street
London W1H 0AH

Dedicated

by gracious permission

to

Her Majesty the Queen of Roumania

*whose love and knowledge of the arts
of the thread have never failed to
encourage fellow needlewomen of all
classes and in many countries*

LIST OF ILLUSTRATIONS

vii

SPECIMENS OF CHURCH WORK

MISCELLANEOUS EXAMPLES

PLATE II
HER MAJESTY AT WORK WITH HER LADIES AT SINAIA

HER MAJESTY'S SHUTTLES

The large one is of mother-of-pearl, the smaller one of opal.

INTRODUCTION

By H.M. THE QUEEN OF ROUMANIA

"WOMAN'S work" has become nowadays a word with such a very different meaning than in former days, that one is nearly obliged to explain what one means. When I say woman's work, I don't mean man's work done by women; I don't mean either the Amazons or the Beehives, as both are unsexed. I mean the work of women who can afford to stay at home, to have ten or twelve children, and be happy in bringing them up to be good, and clever, and useful. For the woman at home this book is written.

The Amazon-woman, the bee-woman, the man-woman need not even open it. But the solitary woman, who has time for reading and thinking—and there are many—may find pleasure in imitating some of our inventions and in adding some inventions in her turn.

To the solitary woman this book does go with the wish to become a companion. Here is pretty work to do during reading—much prettier than knitting. Nowadays work has become a great luxury, as everything useful and necessary is done by machines. Then let the luxury be as beautiful as we can make it. We offer here a kind of lace that long years of constant work have brought us to. It is such quick work—pretty to look at, and centuries won't destroy it. It is quick work for clever fingers, just as the lacemaker's fingers seem to fly, but it takes a great deal of quick working to arrive at making a large piece of lace stuff. But once one is clever enough to read and to work at the same time, it is pleasant indeed. I have known and loved a solitary woman, Miss Fanny Lavater, who used to embroider, as one did in the last century, in petit-point—scenes

B

that look like water-colour painting. And whilst she did that fairy-work she always had a book open before her that she learnt by heart. It was delicious when she spoke about authors: how she could say by heart what they had written.

Nowadays nobody has time to do that, and learning by heart is disdained. My great-aunt, the Princess Louise of Wied, who never married, and who was the great friend of the Queen Adelaide of England, used to learn by heart every day, in order to keep her memory fresh. She wrote poems in English at the age of eighty-six—one very sweet one, " My little room." I don't know if the Amazon and bee-ladies would write a poem about their solitary little room nowadays; the silence of it would become oppressive, as they would not hear the voices of their dear ones talking to them, as my aunt used to do. She sometimes talked to them quite loud.

I have often pitied men—in the first place because they can't know motherhood, in the second, because they are bereft of our greatest comfort—needlework. Our needlework is so much better than their smoking; it is so unobtrusive. Our quiet needle or shuttle, or whatever the instrument may be with which we can produce our modest kind of art, is a true friend, a safe companion, very busy and very discreet. The needle and the shuttle have never betrayed us; the spinning-wheel and the weaving-loom are a little louder, but oh! what a pleasant noise! Even knitting and crochet are a comfort, as it occupies the hands when we feel restless.

What a help when in conversation we do not wish to contradict; we seem to grow silent over some intricate bit of work, and none can guess the little volcano that is covered with the lava of our work.

Some men don't like when the ladies work. It is a mistake. Atavistically we can scarcely help ourselves, as our great-great-great-grandmothers did nothing else. We get into a kind of fever with doing nothing. A very wise country clergyman allowed the women to knit during his sermons; never had a preacher more attentive listeners: not one of them dropped asleep, as overworked women are apt to do when they for once sit down. They grow drowsy and can't keep their eyes open. Allow them to knit or to tat and they will be able to tell you almost every word they have heard.

How much care and sorrow, how much deep anxiety, what profound sorrow and sadness is put into silent woman's work. One ought always to look at it with awe and reverence, not only on account of the patience it teaches, but much more for the silently borne pain it has to hide. Many a woman can say: "What a blessing that my work cannot speak! It would be very startling if it were to lift its voice and begin to reveal the thoughts under whose wing it was hatched.

There is many a tear hidden in woman's work, many a sigh breathed into it, many a word repressed that spoken might have done irretrievable harm.

Luxury—perhaps! But so much more comfort than luxury, so much more rest than the harassing fatigue of bread-winning!

Tatting has the charm of lacemaking and weaving combined. It is the same shuttle as in the weaving-loom, only that the loom is our fingers and the shuttle obeys our thoughts and the invention of the moment. The joy when a new stitch is found is very great. I don't know if Madame Curie felt much happier when she found the Radium! Of course our work is small and modest and will never shake the world. A woman may shake the world once in many centuries, but she can find things in the quiet of her little room that give her complete and intense satisfaction.

Don't despise our needle and our shuttle, don't think that our thoughts need be small for all that! The mothers of very great men could only knit or spin. The weaving of Penelope has become symbolical.

I am atavistically mediæval in my tastes. I love the châtelaine dans son donjon looking out over the lands and working with a lot of laughing and singing maidens weaving and embroidering around her. The minstrel must not be wanting, and the solitude need not be oppressive.

Woman is mostly solitary, even in her household, even doing man's work. Only when she is made into the part of a machine does she stop being a woman.

Is there a prettier picture than a Roumanian peasant girl with her red or orange skirt, a yellow kerchief over her black locks, with dark-fringed large luminous eyes, the green pitcher on her head, walking through the fields and spinning, or the Roumanian woman, draped in the splendid folds of her white or yellow veil, sitting and weaving before her loom?

A woman's hand is never so graceful as when working some lovely piece of art.

Open our book, dear solitary, lonely, worried, or content woman, who is not condemned to earn a hard bread with hard work, and think of the peaceful hours it may bring you, and you will feel that we loved you well in publishing the result of our own loneliness.

CARMEN SYLVA.

Open our book, dear solitary,
lonely, bereaved or content woman,
who is not condemned to earn a hard
bread with hard work, and think of
the peaceful hours it may bring you,
and you will feel that we loved you
well in publishing the result of
our own loneliness.

Carmen Sylva

Feb. 14 10

FACSIMILE OF THE LAST PAGE OF THE QUEEN OF ROUMANIA'S INTRODUCTION

Katharin d Hoare

PLATE III

LADY HOARE AT WORK

THE ART OF TATTING

I HAVE been asked to write a book on tatting, and the word carries me back to early days in my life when my mother, having lost her sight and being a great invalid, took up her shuttle and found great comfort in the art. She was wonderfully clever with her fingers, but found a little difficulty in managing the pin which usually goes with the shuttle of the ordinary pattern. So I invented a shuttle which obviated her having to make use of the pin at all. The shuttle that I had made was of ivory, and rather in the shape of those skate's purses that we, as children, used to pick up on the seashore. One of the legs at either end was longer than the other, and this lengthened leg was used by her as a pin. My love of tatting is therefore inherited. And it has indeed wiled away many hours of illness. To me it has been what I imagine a pipe must be to a man—a companion both in illness and health. I love to sit and read a book whilst my shuttle flies. That others should be enabled to enjoy this pleasant companionship is one of the objects of this book.

Whatever may be its faults, I am indeed fortunate in having a delightful collaborateur—one who has been gracious enough not only to lend me photographs of her beautiful work, but to write the preface for me with her own hand.

Her Majesty the Queen of Roumania, known to many of my readers as "Carmen Sylva," is a mistress in the art of tatting, and has done much, very much, to raise it to a fine art.

Tatting itself is considered in most books on lace or embroidery as scarcely to deserve mention. I am anxious to show that it possesses possibilities of endless adaptation and design.

Many and divers are the reasons given for its name. Some say that it comes from the English word *tatters*, or small pieces; others that it comes from the Indian word *tattie*, an Indian mat, which it is supposed to resemble. But I think a more probable derivation is from an old Icelandic word *taeta*, to teaze, knot, or pick up, or from an old provincial English word *tat*, to entangle, weave, knit, or tat.

The Italians call it *occhi*, from the eye-like shape of the loops. In the East it still bears the name of *makouk*, from the shuttle or *makouk* used in its manufacture.

Whatever be the exact origin of the word, the art can, I think, be traced to *macramé* work, the oldest of all kinds of lace, which is found, for example, in the twisted threads and knotted fringes on the wrappings in the tombs of Upper Egypt, and tatting is only knotting made with a shuttle, and is entirely composed of knots made on a running thread. Mats were made in this way, and, as the work improved, it was seen that a shuttle rendered the work easier. The first work of the kind continued, indeed, to be called *knotting*; it came from Italy in the sixteenth century, and was a variety of the Ragusa or Reticella guipures. Subsequently it came to be known as *punto a groppo*, or *gruppo*, from the fact that the threads are knotted together like the fringed Genoese *macramé*. The fringes on the linen cloths that the Roman peasants wear folded on their heads are work of the same kind. There is an example of this early work in the South Kensington Museum in a sixteenth-century border of knotted threads with a vandyked edge.

Elaborate specimens of *macramé* are still made in the schools and convents of the Riviera, and are carried to great perfection at Chiavari and in the Albergo Dei Poveri at Genoa. *Macramé* is generally the first work taught to children, and is often used for the ends of towels or cloths.

Those who have seen Paolo Veronese's " Last Supper " in the

Louvre may remember that the ends of the table-cloth are done in knotting.

To tatting I can find but few allusions either in English or foreign literature. There is, however, a poem of Sir Charles Sedley's, published in 1707, called *The Royal Knotter*, evidently intended as a skit on William and Mary. The following lines are evidently pointed at the Queen's homely habits, one of which, it is interesting to note, is tatting—

> " Oh happy people ! we must thrive
> Whilst thus the Royal Pair dost strive
>   Both to advance your glory.
> While he (by valour) conquers France,
> She manufactures does advance
>   And makes thread fringes for ye !
>
> Blessed we ! who from such Queens are freed,
> Who by vain superstition led,
>   Are always telling beads.
> For here's a Queen now thanks to God !
> Who when she rides in coach abroad,
>   Is always knotting threads."

Throughout the eighteenth century, although it is seldom actually mentioned, tatting seems to have flourished both in England and France.

In the National Gallery there is a picture, for example, by Sir Joshua Reynolds of the Countess of Albemarle of the day, who is depicted in the act of tatting, shuttle in hand (see Plate IV.).

Of the popularity of tatting in France there is also evidence.

In the Wallace Collection at Hertford House there is one of cut, pierced, and wrought steel with a monogram in flowers that shows that it belonged to Madame Louise, the daughter of Louis XV. If the Princesses of France made it a court accomplishment in the eighteenth century, H.M. the Queen of Roumania has shown that it

is work not unworthy of royal hands in the nineteenth century. There are other shuttles in the same case, veritable masterpieces —one made of rock crystal mounted in gold and set with garnets, another of earlier date of gold of three tints framing beautiful little figure subjects in enamel, a third also of gold in three tints pierced and chased with garlands of leaves tied with bows. These last two, it is interesting to note, are of about the same size and shape as those now used by Her Majesty the Queen.

In Paris there are also some fine specimens of shuttles—probably the finest anywhere—in the Musée de Cluny. One of them is about six inches in length, of gold and red lacquer with a pair of lovers on it in Louis XVI. costume; a second of enamel, rather longer and thinner, green in colour and quite plain design; a third of mother-of-pearl, and much smaller, being only four inches long.

I do not know if these wonderful shuttles worked equally wonderful work. If indeed they did, I fear that we cannot compete with the tatting of past centuries. The plates, however, that follow will show that the art is not altogether dead, nor the faculty for inventing new designs exhausted.

I pass now from these brief historical notes to a few practical suggestions based upon the practice and method that I have for many years adopted.

THE STITCH

First, as to the stitch:—

Make a loop of your thread, as shown in Fig. 1. Hold the join between the first finger and thumb of your left hand, passing the loop over the fingers (see *a*). Let the loose end of the thread hang down, and the end attached to the shuttle remain upwards, passing it over the knuckles of the left hand. Hold the shuttle between the thumb and first finger of the right hand. Put the

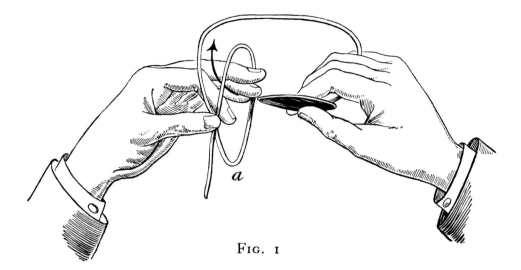

shuttle into the loop, as shown by the arrow, between the first and second fingers of the left hand. Draw the last three fingers of the left hand out of the loop, but keep the finger and thumb still on the join. Pull the thread fastened to the shuttle tight, and by doing so let the half stitch, or knot, be formed by the *loop thread.* Draw the stitch tight by putting the left hand fingers back into the loop and extending them so as to draw the half knot thus formed close to the thumb and finger of the left hand, and complete the half knot thus (in Fig. 2 *b*).

The thread attached to the shuttle will now be hanging down (see Fig. 3) and will not be over the left hand. Keep the left hand as before, with thumb and first finger on join and the other three fingers in the

FIG. 2

loop as before. Hold the shuttle in your right hand, but put it this time over the left hand and beyond the loop (*b*). Now push it backward into the loop between the first and second fingers of the left hand, letting the thread pass under the shuttle between it and the right hand thumb, then back to the left over the shuttle between

C 2

it and the first finger. Do not lose hold of the shuttle in this movement, only raise the finger to let the loop pass under. Take

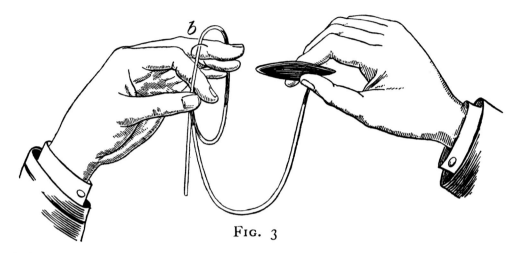

FIG. 3

the left hand fingers out as before, pull your shuttle thread tight so that the knot is formed of the *loop* thread, insert your three left hand fingers again as before into the loop to draw the second part of the knot up to your thumb, and the knot complete is formed.

The figure (No. 4) showing the double or complete stitch is on *e a—b* first part of knot, *c* second part of knot, *d* the loop, *e* a completed stitch drawn up. This is the stitch, and *the error usually made by beginners is that they form the knot of the shuttle thread instead of the loop thread.*

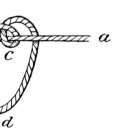

FIG. 4

When you have made sufficient knots draw up your shuttle thread and you will have formed a loop. To make the picots or small loops that stand out from the oval or any part of the design, you merely leave about the eighth of an inch of thread on both loop and shuttle threads before beginning a fresh stitch or knot, as then, when the loop is drawn up, the piece of thread between the stitch or knot will stand out like a small loop or picot, as it is called. You must always divide your picots by making a stitch or more between them, and you must be careful always to leave the same length of thread between the stitches. You join your ovals together by these picots.

Tatting with two shuttles is very simple. Instead of making a loop to begin with, you knot your two threads together, and then

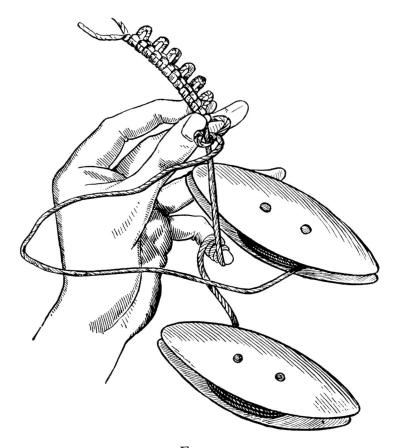

FIG. 5

twist the thread of one shuttle round the little finger of your left hand, making the knots as before of this thread, and using your second shuttle in your right hand as directed in the explanations of single tatting. Fig. 5 will explain this.

A beginner will do well to practise with a piece of smooth twine.

PLATE V

HER MAJESTY THE QUEEN AT WORK ON A VEIL TO COVER A VERY
ANCIENT BIBLE

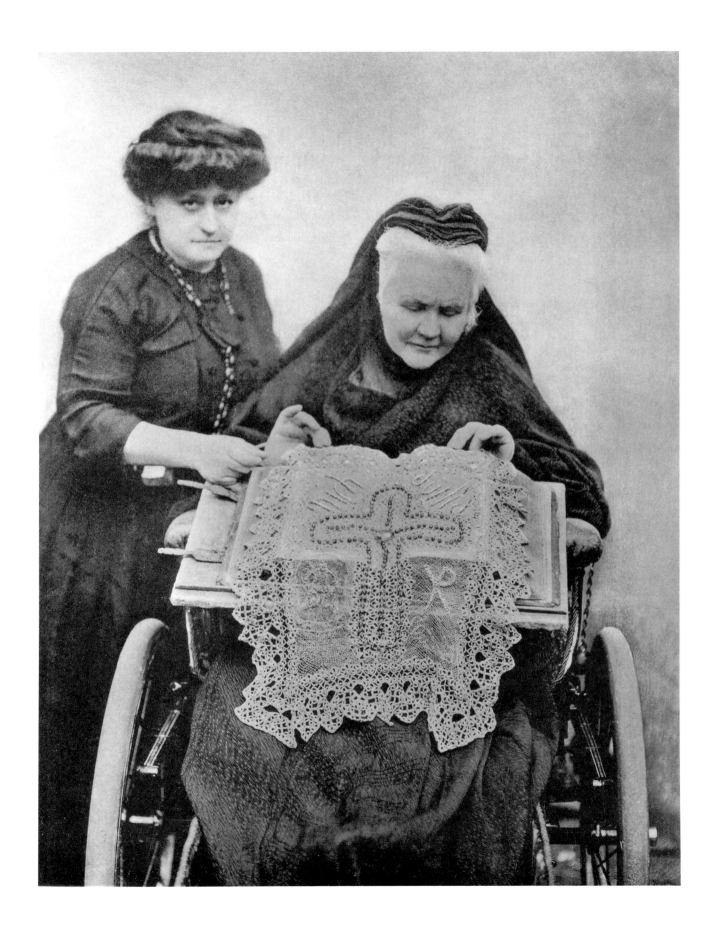

THE THREAD

Next, thread evenly spun is far better for use than cotton, and this can now be easily procured in many colours. The Dolfus Mieg [1] Company's catalogue of articles for work gives a long list of flax spun in varying degrees of fineness and colour which tat well and easily. Silk also is an excellent material to use, and the same company sell most beautiful silks in good colours. It is also easier to tat in silk than in thread. Her Majesty the Queen of Roumania has made very beautiful designs, using two shades of white silk—a blue white and a cream white. This she further enriches with gold thread and jewels.

The Dolfus Mieg Company's gold thread is very good for tatting. As to tatting in gold or silver thread, let me say in passing that you must use two shuttles, one with the gold or silver thread, on the other a rather thick thread or silk, the latter being the running thread, as you cannot easily pull up gold or silver thread.

DESIGNS

Thirdly, as to patterns and designs:

In all the notices on tatting that I can find there seems to be no idea that anything but circles, ovals, or adaptation of circles can be made. But with two shuttles and an inventive brain, there is no end to the designs that may be invented. For instance, it occurred to me as I worked that tatting would appliqué well on to fine net. The plates will show if I have succeeded.

Tatting also adapts itself easily to church work. Markers look exceedingly well with good tatting designs in any coloured silk, or even in cream thread outlined in gold.

After giving these few directions with reference to the stitch and the thread, I now proceed to describe some photographs of certain

[1] Dolfus Mieg et Cie, Mulhaus, Alsace, Germany.

work and designs which seem to me to illustrate the possibilities of tatting.

Most of the more elaborate designs are worked with two shuttles, in order that straight lines may be made, for, obviously, designs made with one thread must be oval or round in shape, whereas working with two shuttles you are not forced to draw up your thread, but can go on as long in any direction as you may desire. The Queen of Roumania has devised a very clever method of even with one shuttle getting from one part of a pattern to another so as to avoid breaking off your thread. To do this she has a small hook on a chain fastened to her dress, and she draws the thread with the hook along through the stitches behind until she reaches the desired spot. By this means she can begin her pattern again; or if she is working with two shuttles, she passes one thread back and forward between the stitches made by the other shuttle until again the desired spot is reached. In this manner knots and joins can be avoided, a result greatly to be desired.

As the reader will see, all Her Majesty's patterns have been reproduced with her own explanations.

EXAMPLES OF THE QUEEN OF ROUMANIA'S WORK

Plate VI

Coverlet made for the Baby Son of the Crown Prince

For beauty of design and fineness of tatting and needlework, I venture to think that it surpasses all the specimens of Her Majesty's work that I have had the good fortune to see.

Description by the Queen.—In the centre, *Nani, nani-bobociluli* (Hush thee, bonny Baby).

Emblems all round of what the baby should possess—*Heartsease, Palms, Edelweiss, Cross* (for bravery), *Laurels*, and at the four corners four angels, meaning—

> Four corners to my bed,
> Four angels round my head,
> One to watch and one to pray,
> And two to bear my soul away.

PLATE VII

Altar Veil with Pearls tatted into the Design

Description by the Queen.—Chalice cover in very fine white silk with real pearls. The silk thread is drawn through the pearls with a hair and then tatted into the work, not put on afterwards.

Plate VIII

Coverlet on Roumanian Crêpe

The Queen, it should be noticed, frequently tats in silk of about the thickness of our purse silk, and often uses more than one colour. The photographs of this bedcover for her niece illustrate this work in colours, though it gives but a poor idea of the effect of the two shades, blue white and cream white of the somewhat coarse silk.

The coverlet is made of a fine kind of Roumanian crêpe, composed of cotton woven by the peasants, and the heavy tatting has an excellent effect upon it. It is altogether about two yards and a half long and about one yard and a half in width, and contains about eighteen or twenty different designs.

Description by the Queen.—A bedcover for my invalid niece made of the finest Roumanian *Panza*. The tatting is done in thick white knitting silk. The seams of the material are joined by tatting. Many of the designs of the border were taken from marble sculptures.

PLATE IX

VARIOUS PORTIONS OF THE COVERLET

In Plates IX and X can be seen the endless variety of patterns that the Queen has used, and when it is remembered that each pattern is worked in two shades, the skill and beauty of the work will be realised.

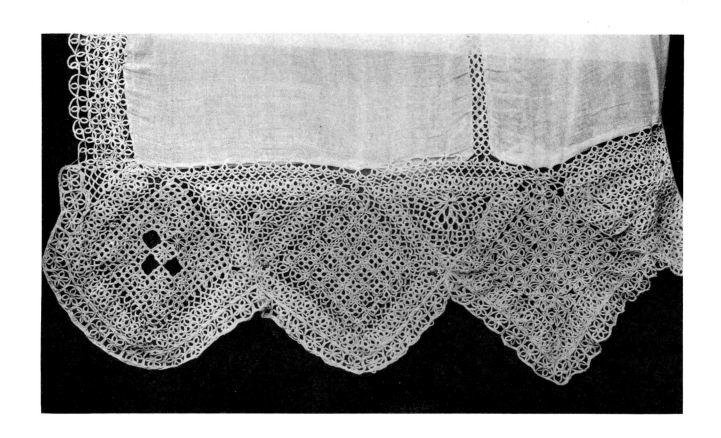

PLATE X

VARIOUS PATTERNS ON THE COVERLET BY THE QUEEN

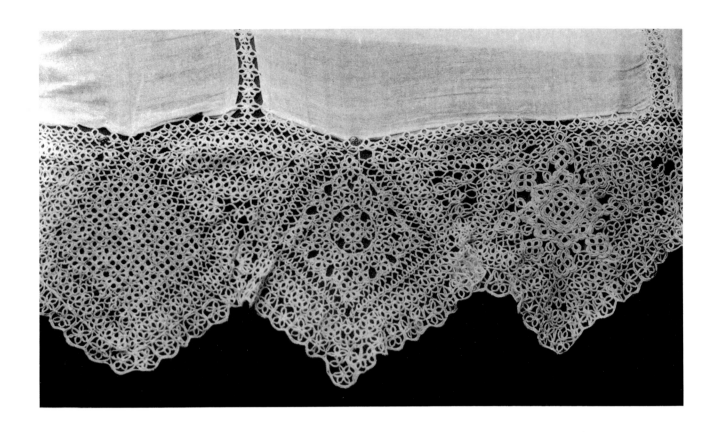

PLATE XII

CHALICE VEIL WORKED IN THICK WHITE SILK AND OVER-SEWN IN
PLACES IN BUTTONHOLE STITCH AND WITH A BORDER OF
CRYSTAL DROPS.

Description by the Queen.—Chalice cover in white silk embroidered
with crystals for a church.

PLATE XIII

DRESS TRIMMING

Front of a dress trimming for H.R.H. the Princess Elizabeth of Roumania. Attention should be called to the curious art of the centre where the work has been entirely done with the shuttle. The edging is in silver.

Description by the Queen.—Bodice tatted in fine white silk for my niece Elizabeth of Roumania. Front and back are made with one uninterrupted thread. The lace stitch in the middle is also done with the shuttle and the same thread.

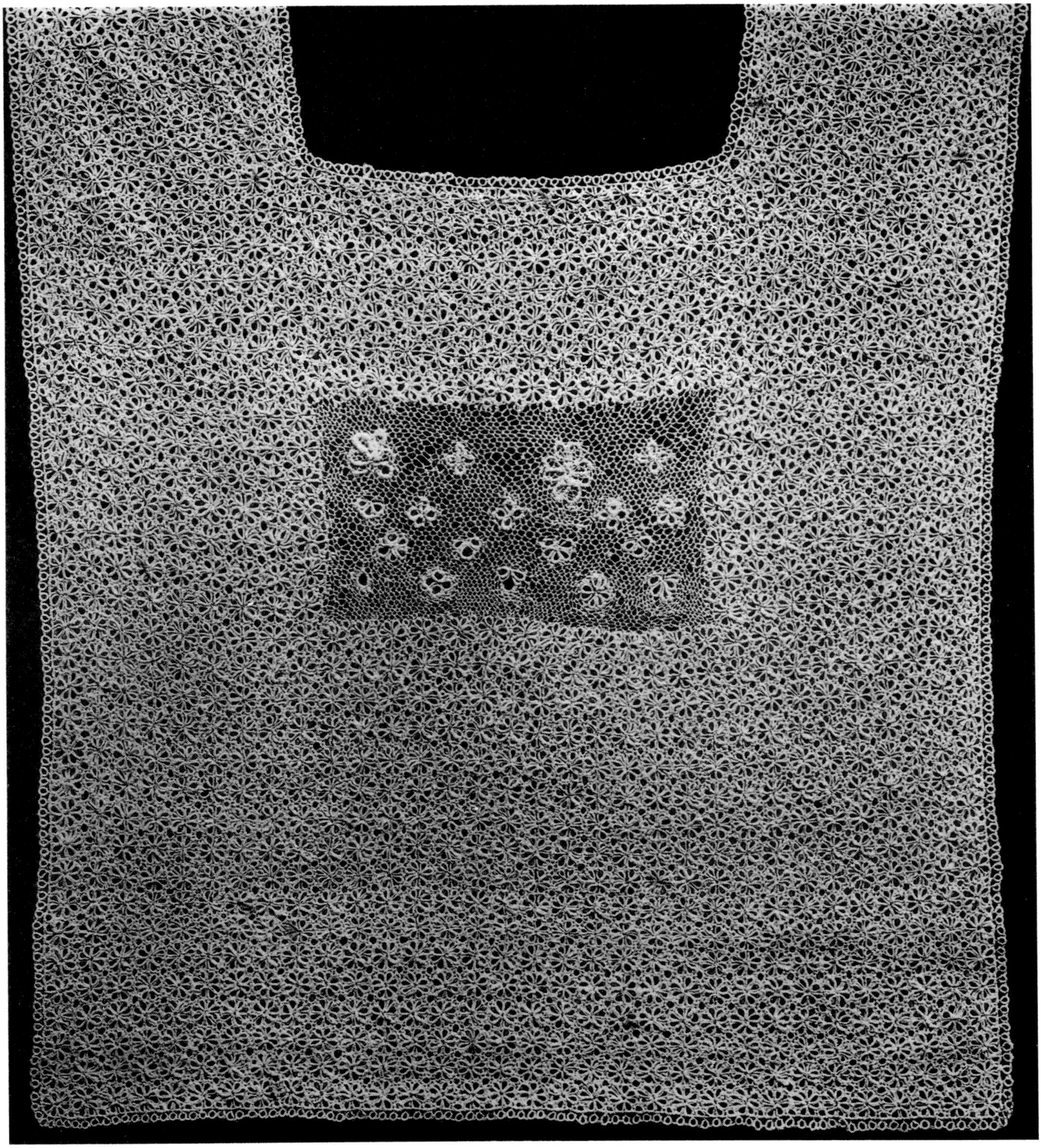

PLATE XIV

DRESS TRIMMING

The back of the same bodice.

Plate XV

Curtain for Iconostasis

This is the largest piece of work that Her Majesty has undertaken. With its adornment of turquoises and topazes, and its background of gold thread, it is needless to add how magnificent is the result.

Description by the Queen.—A curtain for the door of the Iconostasis in the Church of Sinaia, two metres long, tatted in yellow-brown silk. The Byzantine cross is embroidered over in buttonhole stitch with a topaz in each marguerite. The background, as it is begun in the right corner, is embroidered in gold thread in lace stitch, and every marguerite has a turquoise in the middle.

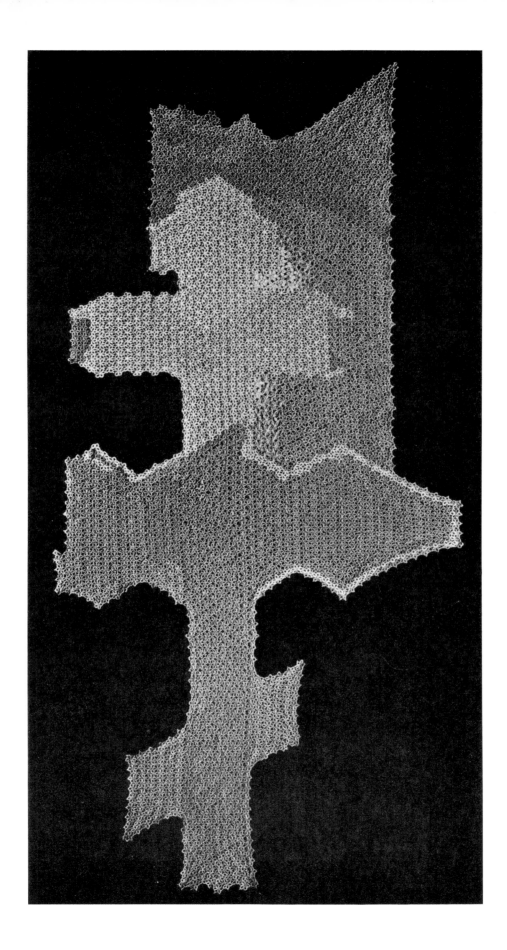

Plate XVI

Chalice Veil in Gold and Needlework and Tatting enriched with many Jewels and surmounted by a raised Cross

The cross is made in metal enriched with jewels, and round the veil in old Roumanian lettering is " Have mercy upon us, O God, after Thy great goodness."

Description by the Queen.—Chalice cover, one metre in diameter. Ground work in gold thread in needlepoint. Letters in gold and pearls. Centre of flowers being turquoises. Surmounted with a cross in metal, pearls.

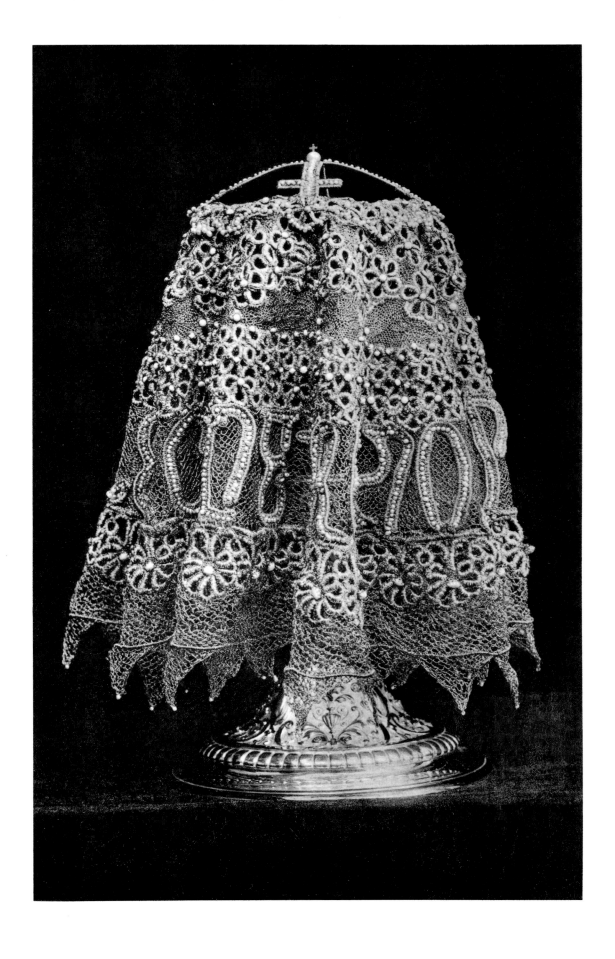

PLATE XVII

ANOTHER VIEW OF THE SAME

PLATE XVIII

LETTER J TATTED BY THE QUEEN IN GOLD THREAD

It may be noted that this is tiresome work, as the gold thread is apt to cut the fingers. The best gold to use is either that used for military embroidery, or the fine gold thread sold by the Dolfus Mieg Company.

Description by the Queen.—Done with two threads, silk underneath, gold at the top, tatted, not embroidered, natural size.

PLATE XIX

Cover in White Silk Tatting, for covering Glass of Water
in a new Three-cornered Stitch

PLATE XX

Description by the Queen.—Sack bag for the Princess of Roumania, worked entirely in gold thread with Topazes.

SPECIMENS OF LADY HOARE'S WORK AND
DESIGNS

Plate XXI

Simple Insertions and Patterns

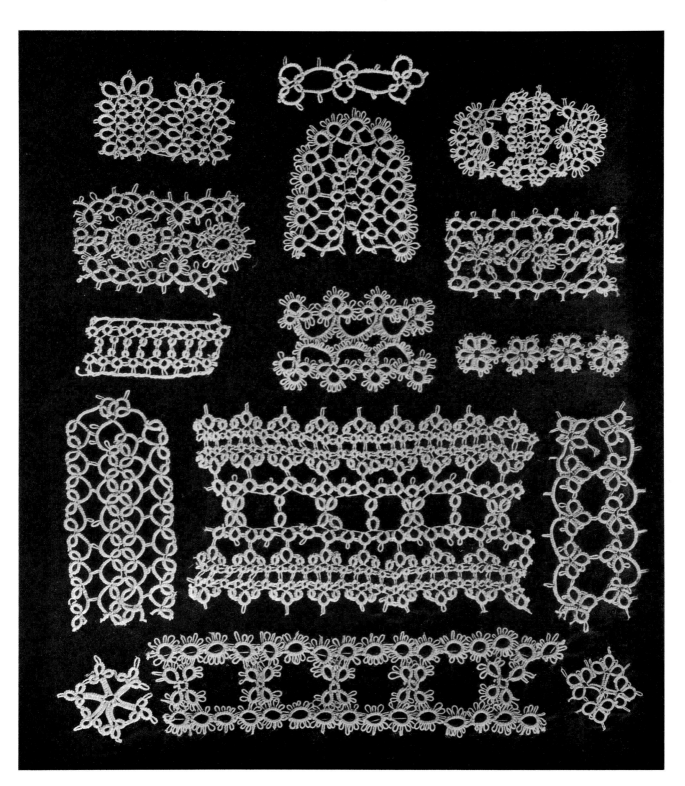

PLATE XXII

SIMPLE INSERTIONS AND PATTERNS

PLATE XXIII

SIMPLE INSERTIONS AND PATTERNS

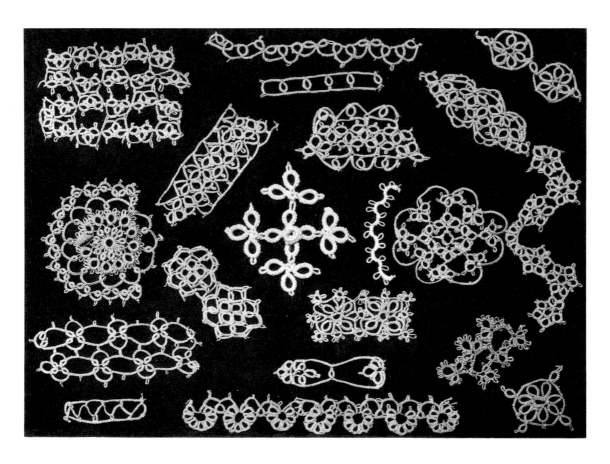

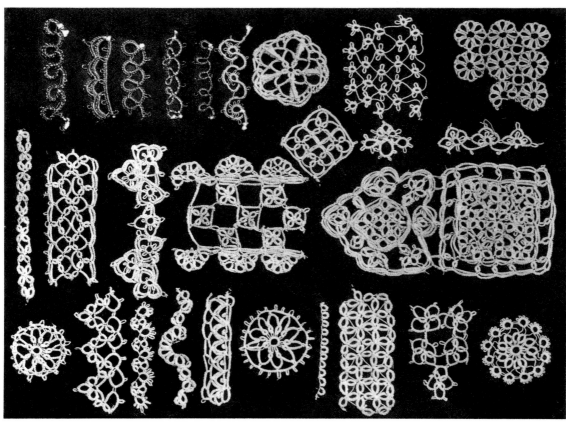

PLATE XXIV

SIMPLE INSERTIONS AND PATTERNS

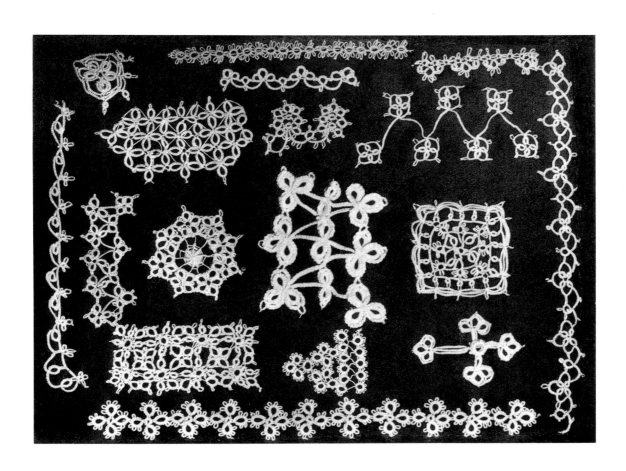

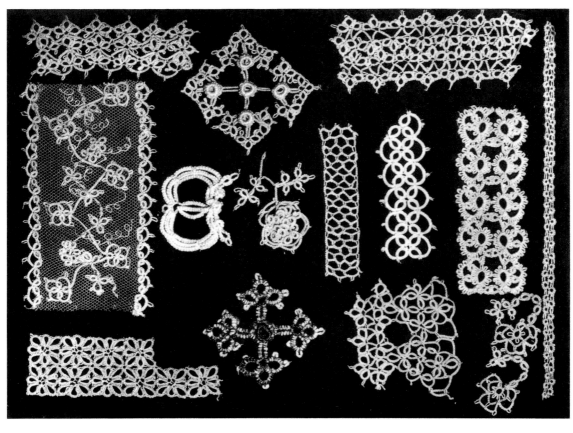

PLATE XXV

A—HALF OF COLLAR FOR A DRESS. This is my first piece of appliqué on Brussels net. The idea came to me that tatting so applied would look well. The collar and sleeves are all done in single tatting with only one shuttle.

Only half the collar shown.

B—COLLAR FOR A BLOUSE, appliqué, with black velvet ribbon run in and mostly composed of rosettes of tatting. This requires but one shuttle.

PLATE XXVI

FLOUNCE APPLIQUÉ ON NET

This flounce was one of my earliest attempts of appliquéd work.

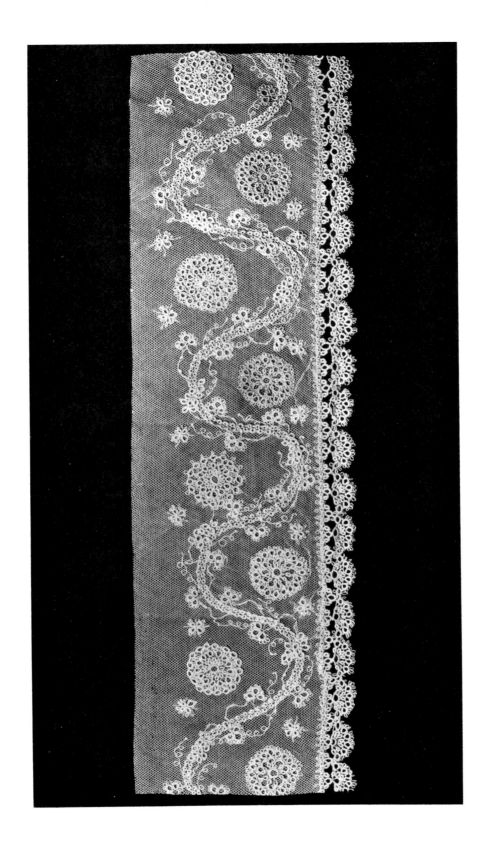

Plate XXVII

Collar of an old shape, the material of which is fine Irish cambric. The tatting was done with two shuttles.

PLATE XXVIII

SQUARE OF APPLIQUÉ, worked for the most part with two shuttles. The idea of this design I got from a piece of Alençon semé with the Napoleonic Bees, made for Napoleon I. as a gift for the Empress Josephine. The little falling tassels were done with the needle.

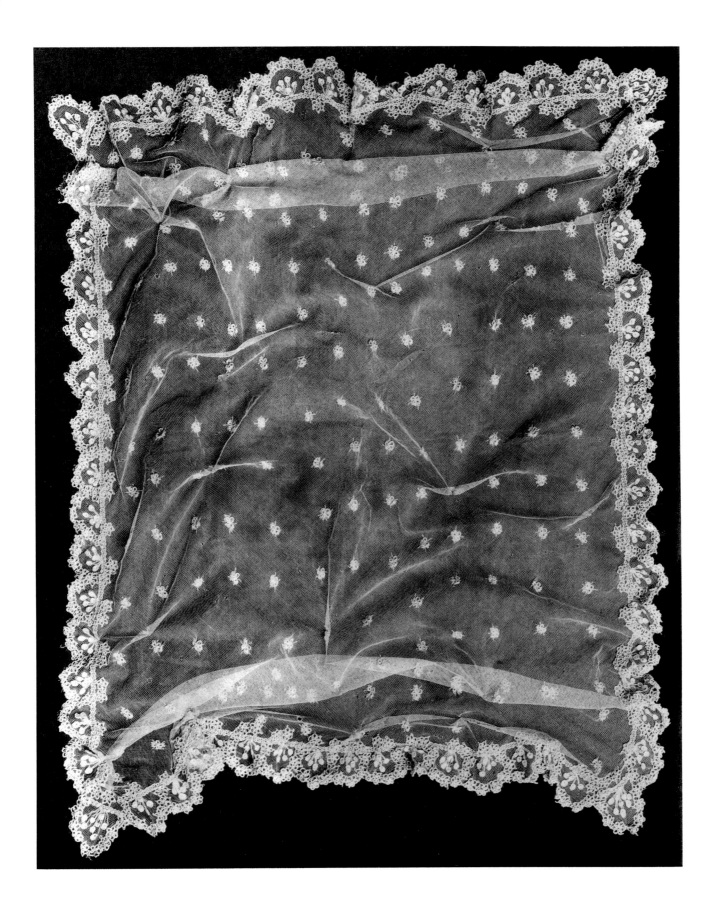

Plate XXIX

Bolero, in single tatting, worked, as indeed nearly all my tatting is worked, in unbleached thread so that its colour should be that of old lace. It should be noted that a design of this kind looks best with a background of soft coloured stuff.

The thread I get through Miss Moody, 54 Sloane Square. It is very smooth, is spun in Scotland, and called Knox's *linen gimp*. The size with which I usually work is No. 24. Both finer and coarser thread of this kind can be obtained.

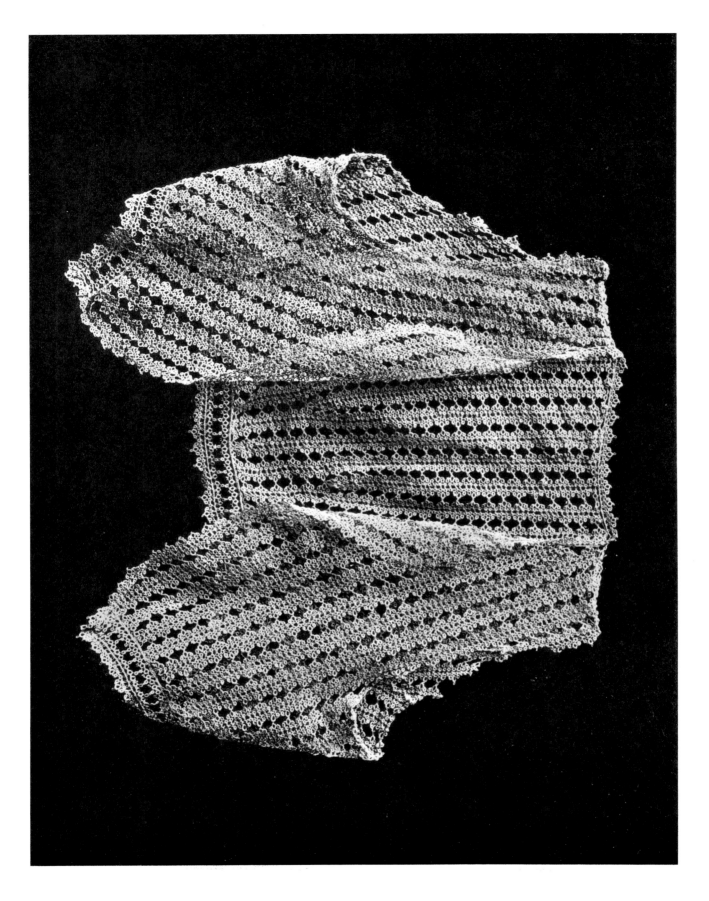

PLATE XXX

COLLAR, on fine Irish cambric, tatted mostly with two shuttles, the roses and foliage, which are appliquéd on it, being in single tatting. The shape is taken from a picture of my husband's grandmother by George Richmond.

PLATE XXXI

SCARF, on fine Brussels net. The tatting is done mostly with two shuttles.

Design, rosettes connected by branching stems, which are crossed in lattice fashion, edge of trefoils.

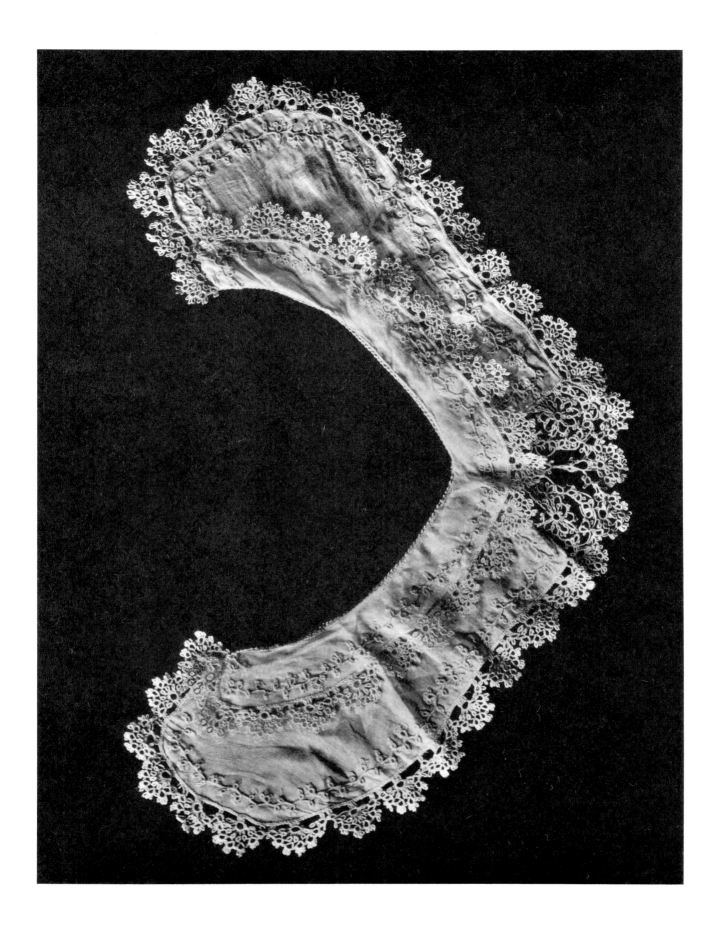

TRIMMING FOR AN EVENING DRESS, of single tatting on fine net, the spots being put in by hand.

Plate XXXIV

A—LETTER CASE, made of unbleached hand-made linen with a design of roses and scrolls in single tatting.

B—CARD CASE, made in double tatting over cream satin, with a needlework border. This pattern can be worked without breaking the thread as the design is done up and down.

Plate XXXV

Berthe for a Low Dress, or a trimming for a high dress. The tatting is in fine thread on Brussels net, spotted by hand.

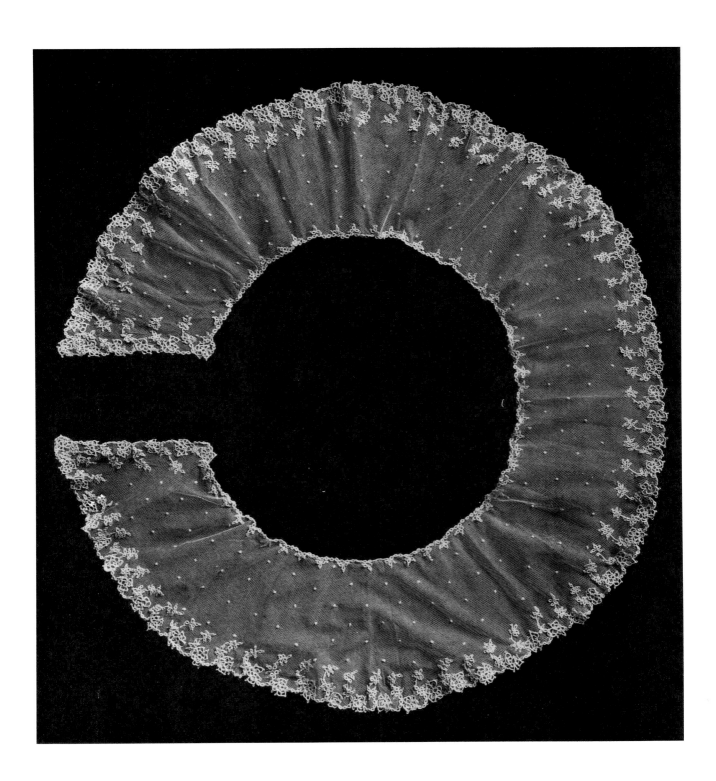

PLATE XXXVI

TRIMMING FOR A DRESS, in thread, with two shuttles. The design is after the manner of Greek lace or the Italian *Tagliato*.

PLATE XXXVII

HAND-BAG, in black moiré lined with white satin. The tatting
design in thread is both in single and double.

PLATE XXXVIII

FICHU, with designs of lilies and roses done with two shuttles in thread on finest net, of small mesh.

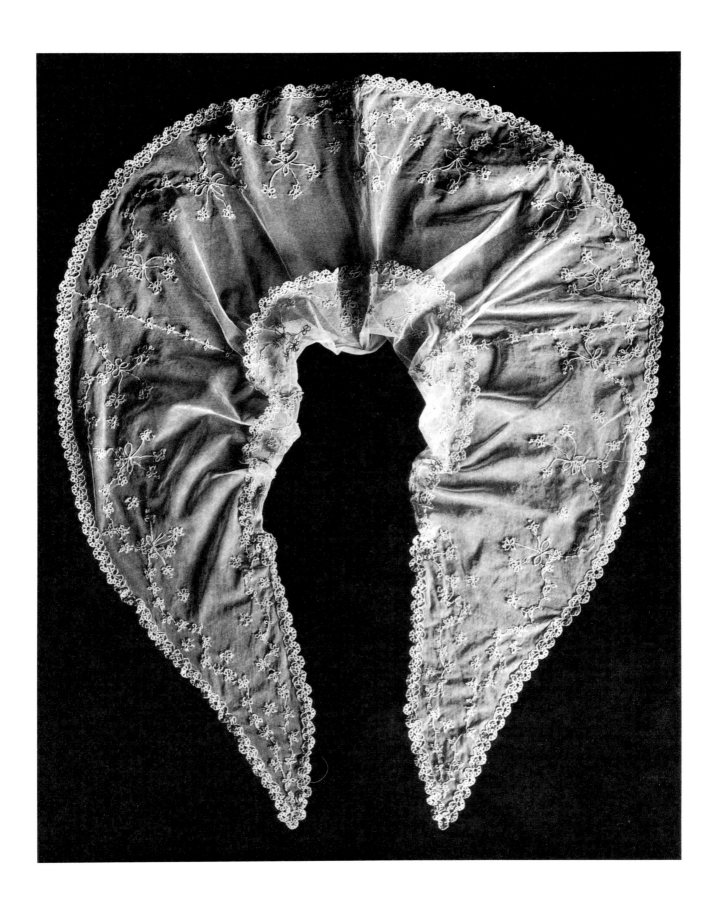

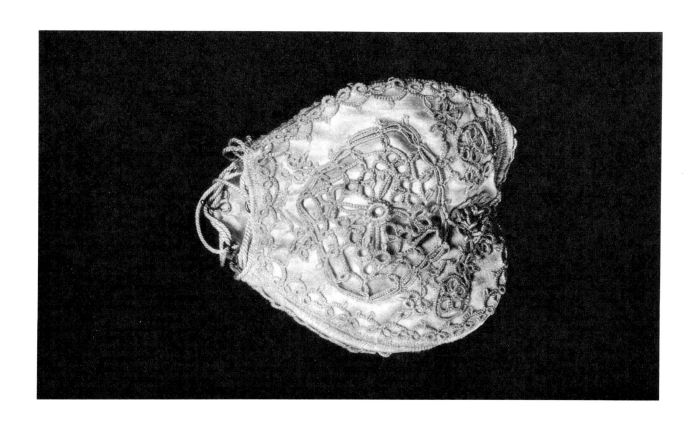

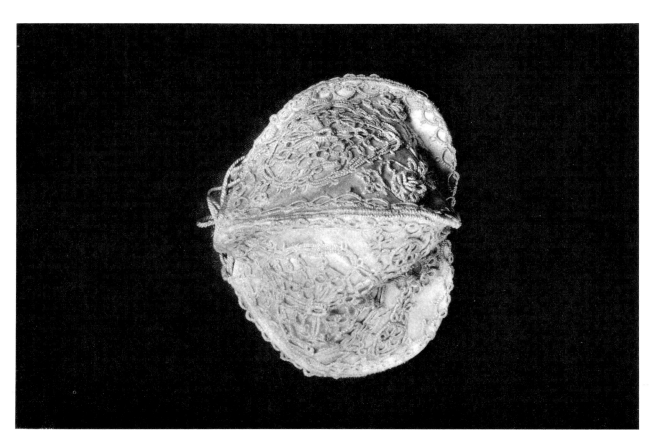

PLATE XL

SCARF, of black net, with the design taken from a piece of old Alençon in green linen thread. The drops are in crimson thread. Above the three rows of scroll work the net is sprinkled with green bees with red legs. The edge is of gold and a gold thread runs through the pattern.

PLATE XLI

CAP, on two kinds of net. The design, roses and leaves, in linen thread.

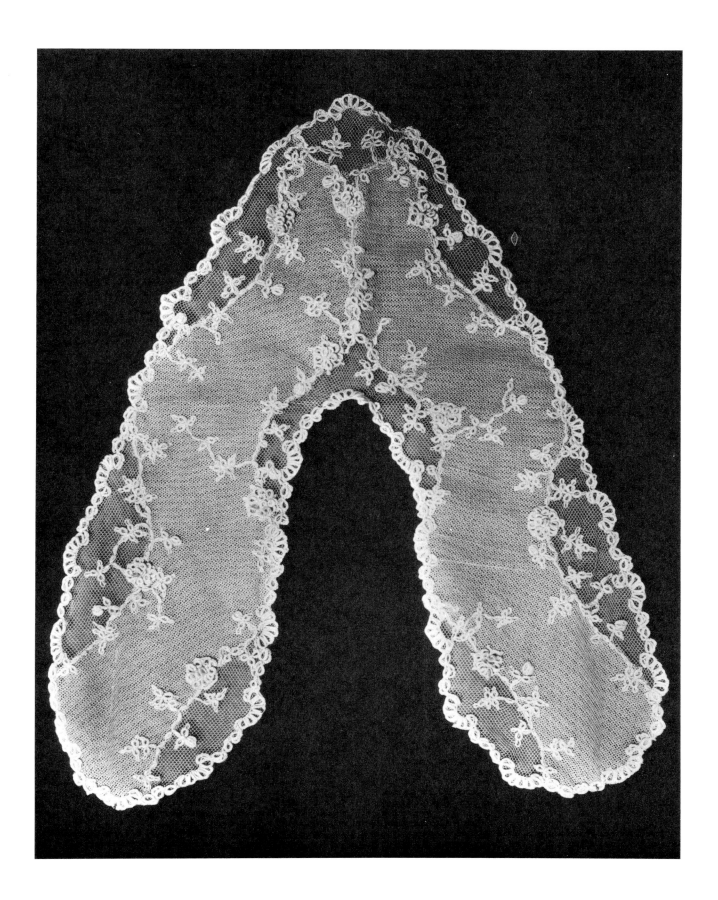

PLATE XLII

A—INSERTION. The design of pomegranates and acorns is in linen thread.

B—SCARF, in fine Roumanian crêpe with the border in squares of tatting of varied designs, divided by a tatting insertion, and edged with a border of vandykes.

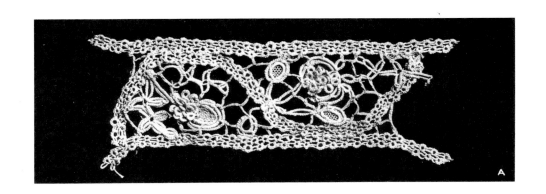

PLATE XLIII

WAISTCOAT, in white silk with tatting in natural coloured thread.

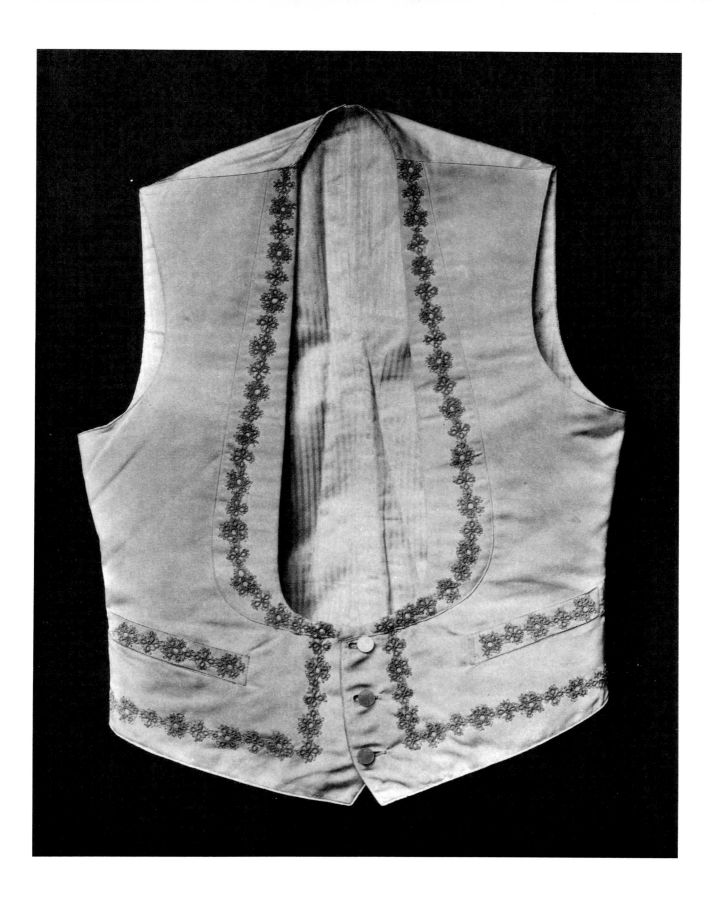

Plate XLIV

A—Shuttle in Ivory invented by me for my mother.
The extra length of one of the prongs at each end serves as a pin.

B—Knotting—Sixteenth Century

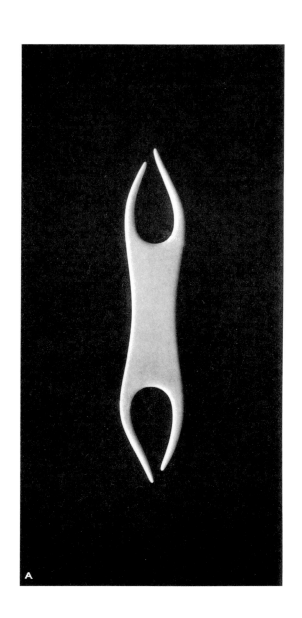

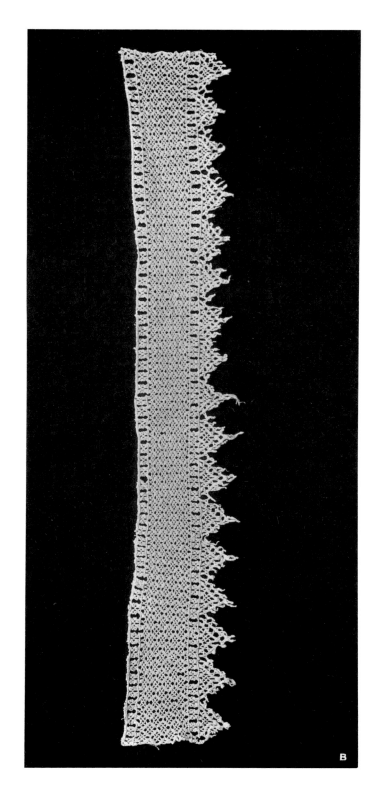

SPECIMENS OF CHURCH WORK

PLATE XLV

MARKERS

1. On cream ribbon, tatting in pale blue-green thread outlined in gold.
2. Red ribbon, design in cream thread outlined with gold.
3. Green ribbon, design in cream thread outlined with gold.
4. Green ribbon with tudor rose.
5. Purple ribbon, design in cream outlined in gold.

PLATE XLVI

CHALICE VEIL, in two kinds of net, tatted in fine thread with a design of vine leaves, grapes, roses, and leaves, and a border of crosses.

The centre is fine French cambric with the cross tatted in thread and a needlework border.

Plate XLVII

Chalice Veil, of fine Brussels net, worked in fine thread, with a design of vine leaves, tendrils, and grapes in clusters.

PLATE XLVIII

THE SAME VEIL PLACED OVER CHALICE

Plate XLIX

Chalice Veil, two kinds of net, design vine leaves, tendrils and grapes, with roses and leaves.

Centre fine cambric, tatting cross and needlework edging.

PLATE L

MANIPLE in red silk. The crosses are done in two shades of red thread, the centres being deep red, the border of a lighter shade, edged with gold.

MISCELLANEOUS EXAMPLES

Plate LI

Shuttles in Wallace Collection

By the kind permission of the Keeper of the Wallace Collection I am able to give reproductions of these interesting shuttles.

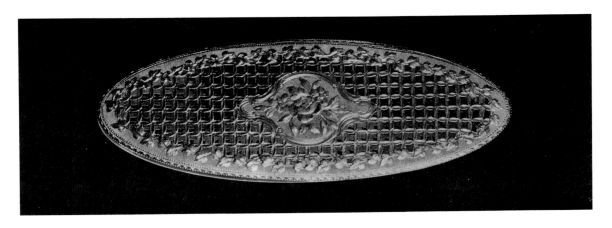

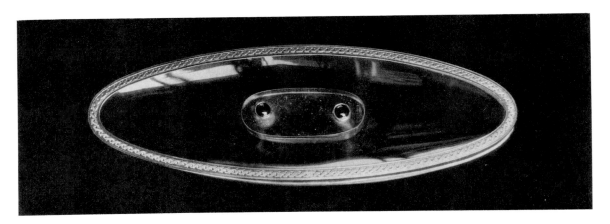

PLATE LII

Baby's Robe made by my mother, who was blind. The tatting is of several designs, and looks exceedingly well over a white satin petticoat. This tatting was made in 1866. The edging is filled in with needlework.

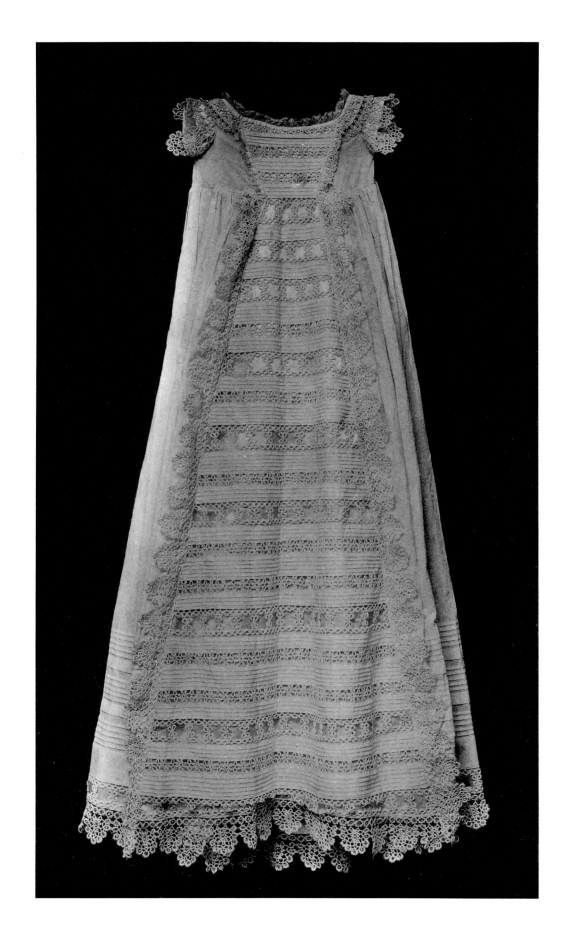

PLATE LIII

Irish Tatting in the Victoria and Albert Museum, made at Ardee in 1880, with a wheel design and needlework centres.

Kindly sent me by the Director.

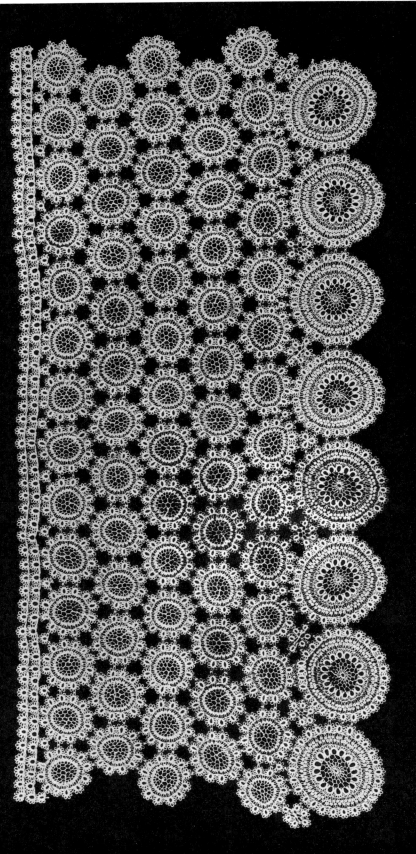

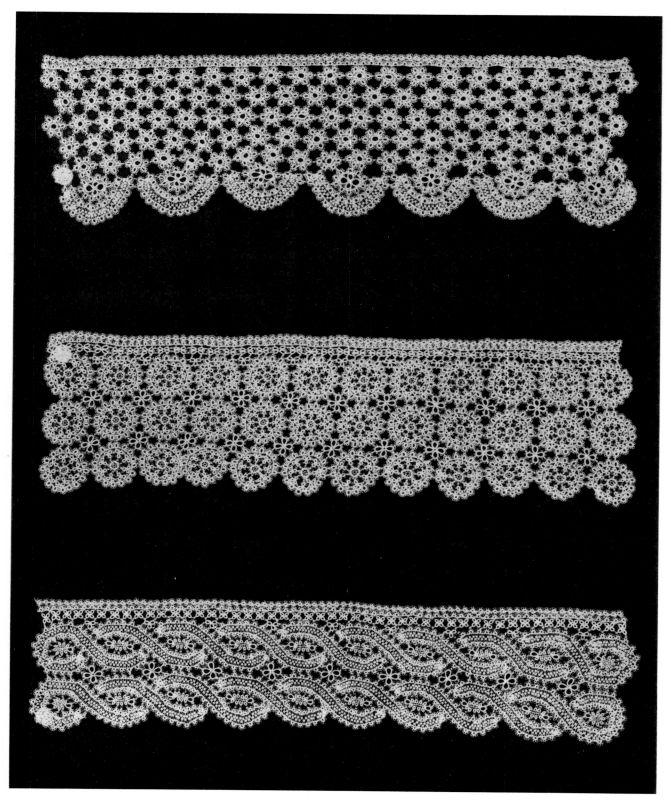

PLATE LIV

TATTING in the Royal Scottish Museum, Edinburgh.
Kindly sent me by the director.